Becoming Hank Moody: Get the Style, Confidence, and Girls and Live Life Like Hank Moody

L. A. MOORE

Although the author and publisher have made every effort to ensure that the information in this book was correct at press time, the author and publisher do not assume and hereby disclaim any liability to any party for any loss, damage, or disruption caused by errors or omissions, whether such errors or omissions result from negligence, accident, or any other cause.

This book is presented solely for educational and entertainment purposes. This book is designed to provide information and motivation to our readers. It is sold with the understanding that the publisher is not engaged to render any type of psychological, legal, or any other kind of professional advice. The content of each article is the sole expression and opinion of its author, and not necessarily that of the publisher. No warranties or guarantees are expressed or implied by the publisher's choice to include any of the content in this volume. Neither the publisher nor the individual author(s) shall be liable for any physical, psychological, emotional, financial, or commercial damages, including, but not limited to, special, incidental, consequential or other damages. Our views and rights are the same: You are responsible for your own choices, actions, and results. This book is not intended as a substitute for the medical advice of physicians.

For my Karen.

CONTENTS

ACKNOWLEDGMENTS

Californication, Hank Moody, and just about every other reference in this book are trademarks of Showtime Networks Inc. Without them, there would be no Californication, and thus, no book. The show is great, and this book isn't intended to breach any rights, trademarks or laws. I'm sure Showtime's lawyers are awesome and understand, just like you do, that this book is intended to inform, educate, and express opinions, which incidentally is protected under the First Amendment to the U.S. Constitution.

1 MY NAME IS HANK

The sun is beating down on the Hollywood Forever Cemetery and a lone 1991 Porsche 964 Cabriolet approaches the imposing religious architecture. Approaching the Church at the end of the driveway, sprinklers keep the grass looking green on either side of the road. Whilst the imagery and symmetry is unadulterated, the same cannot be said for the driver of the car. A dishevelled character steps out of the driver's side, a cigarette dangling precariously from his lips, as he lifts his sunglasses to gaze upon the setting. Squinting, his eyes attempt to adjust to the light after one too many drinks the night before.

He makes his way inside the Church, designed by Ezra F Kysor and W J Mathews. Throwing his cigarette butt into the Holy water, he manages disregard both religion and two of America's first practising architects of the 19th Century in one vulgar effort.

"Ok, big guy, you and me. We've never done this before, but desperate times call for desperate measures." Making his way down the aisle, he looks up towards the representation of Christ, their faces both offering a look of destitution. "My name is Hank."

Of course, I'm referring to the opening scenes of the pilot episode of Californication. It was the first time I'd encountered Hank Moody, and like many other thousands who have watched each episode since then, it was the beginning of a character relationship that developed to a level that I could not foresee. Despite the obvious continuity errors for those knowledgeable of Los Angeles religious architecture (the exterior shots were filmed at Hollywood Forever Cemetery, whilst the interior shots were filmed at the former Cathedral of Saint Vibiana) the character of Hank immediately gripped most viewers by the bollocks, gently massaging them, captivating you.

In this book I take a closer look at the character of Hank Moody, analysing everything from his lifestyle, to his outlook on life and religion, before offering real, actionable advice that can be implemented by anybody who wishes to pursue, or even replicate such a life.

Before researching Hank's character for this book, I really thought I knew him. I thought writing a book on becoming him would just be a simple case of explaining how to be a confident person who doesn't care too much about embarrassing oneself, and how to create a life for yourself doing whatever you want, whenever you want. In reality, I couldn't have been further from the truth, as we'll see as we start to deconstruct Hank's character.

In a similar fashion to Hank though, I don't give a fuck

if you like it or not. It's my musings on a character that I've come to love and hate over a number of series. Take it or leave it, motherfucker!

2 HOW HANK WAS BORN

"I'm the conduit through which America views the soft underbelly of women's erotic desires."

Somebody once told me to write for the person that hasn't got a clue what you're talking about. With that being said, I will now briefly explain *Californication* and David Duchovny, the actor who plays Hank Moody in the show, to my mother. Quite why I'm doing this I've yet to figure out, as who would really buy a book about becoming a guy they've never heard of? In fact, I'm rather tempted to exclude this section from the book, just so they continue to have no fucking idea what the show is about. But that would be mean. Very mean. And I'm not that kind of guy.

Californication is an American TV show created by Tom Kapinos. It debuted on Showtime on August 13th 2007. The story revolves around a writer, Hank Moody (played by David Duchovny), who is in the midst of a personal crisis. The show portrays his sexual escapades, a stranded relationship with his ex, his daughter and other people in his life, as well as his work, writer's block and legal troubles.

The show has been very well received by both critics and the audience. As of June 2013, *Californication* has run for six seasons, with the seventh going into production later this year and is expected to be first aired in 2014.

Hank Moody is a talented writer who moves from New York to LA seeking fame and fortune. What he finds however is less than pleasing. He is unable to resist temptation, especially if it's in a form of an attractive woman. This leads him to enter into all sorts of sexual escapades that don't always end that well. Well, the sexual escapades tend to end well, it's what happens as a result of them, or just after the climax, so to speak. His life is in a mess: he is an alcoholic and unable to focus on his work or people around him. This crisis is particularly evident when it comes to close people in his life. At the beginning of the show, his ex, Karen (Natascha McElhone) is about to marry another man. It is clear Hank is still yearning for Karen, but is unable to prove he is mature enough for a monogamous relationship. Another stranded relationship in Hank's life is with his teenage daughter, Becca (Madeleine Martin), who is slowly discovering the exciting world of parties and sex. In addition to this, Hank has huge problems with his work;

he's troubled by a major writer's block, which only makes him indulge in alcohol and drugs more.

Californication is a fast, exciting show full of strong language, witty dialogue, sex, drugs and rock n' roll. Through its six seasons, we follow Hank as he tries to fight his personal demons and get his life back on track.

For the benefit of my own mother, and others stupid enough to buy a book about a TV character they have no idea about, here is a brief overview of some of the key characters within *Californication*.

Hank Moody (David Duchovny)

A talented but problematic writer with alcohol and drug problems. He is a careless womanizer and he can't say 'no' to pleasures, which often gets him in scandalous situations. His writing is also suffering from this crisis.

Karen Van der Beek (Natasha McElhone)

Hank's long-term on-and-off girlfriend. At the beginning of the show she is about to marry another man. Hank is still in love with her but their relationship is complex. She is the mother of his daughter, Becca.

Becca Moody (Madeleine Martin)

Hank and Karen's teenage daughter. Hank has a complicated and often stranded relationship with her.

Charlie Runkle (Evan Handler)

Hank's best friend, agent, Runkle is a full-time masterbator.

Marcy Runkle (Pamela Adlon)

Charlie's on-and-off nymphomaniac wife.

Bill Lewis (Damian Young)

Karen's fiancé in season 1 and Hank's great enemy. He has a teenage daughter, Mia.

Mia Lewis (Madeline Zima)

Bill's teen daughter and writer with a pen name Mia Cross. Hank has a one night stand with her without knowing her true age and identity. Oops.

Beatrice (Trixie) (Judy Geer)

A high-end prostitute who is also Hank's friend.

Todd Carr (Chris Williams)

The director of the movie adaptation of Hank's book "God Hates Us All".

Lew Ashby (Callum Keith Rennie)

A producer who approaches Hank with a book deal (to write his biography).

Whilst that offers a nice overview of the main characters, it's one man in particular we are interested in here. This isn't *'Becoming Karen Van der Beek',* although I'd like to claim the copyright on that one too before you go penning your own book. Cheeky bastard.

David Duchovny plays Hank Moody, the star of Showtime's hit series, *Californication.* No stranger to the screen, Duchovny also played Fox in *The X-Files* all those years ago, which is perhaps why, like me, you sat staring at the screen for the entire first episode wondering how the fuck you know Hank Moody. In parts, I thought I was looking into the eyes of my real father for the first time – at least that is how I expect such a reaction to feel like. I have known my father since birth, so I can't really say for sure though.

Born in 1960, Duchovny originally hails from New York City, where he attended Grace Church School and The Collegiate School for Boys. He attended Princeton University, from which he graduated in 1982 with a Bachelor of Arts in English Literature. Not one to shy away from further education, he then went on to complete a Master of Arts in English Literature at Yale University, although his subsequent attempt at a PhD still remains unfinished. I guess that's proof enough he is in fact human.

David was born to a Scottish mother who worked at a local school as an administrator and teacher. His determination to peruse his childhood dreams of becoming a superstar artist was inspired by his father who was a writer and publicist for the American Jewish.

David Duchovny's parents separated when he was only eleven years old and life was never the same afterwards. Being the family's middle child, his mother could not leave him stay with the father. She opted to take him with her plus his other two siblings. According to him, this was one of the driving forces that gave him the power to achieve.

Duchovny began his school life at the Collegiate School in Manhattan where he had secured a scholarship. By then, he used to live uptown. Due to her mother's economic predicaments, David had to go the extra mile to make the ends meet. He, unlike his classmates, used to do odd jobs to fetch something for the family. His perseverance at work mentored him a lot to become what he is today. He first worked as a bicycle delivery person and later as a lifeguard during summer breaks.[1] Despite this challenging life, David had made it clear in his mind that achievement was his destiny. His hard work saw him graduate from high school ready for another more challenging life ahead. His education didn't ended there either. His passion to become a renowned artist gave him the much-needed hope which saw him pursue a Bachelor of Arts in literature at Princeton University.

David was able to enrol for a master's degree and it is during this time that good things started coming his way. In fact he was a big enough risk taker to abandon his thesis when he had started to travel to New York to act in Broadways plays. Although his mother raised strong objection to this, David had other things in mind. To become rock-star in Hollywood!

The acting life of David dates back to 1987 when he first appeared in an advisement for Lowenbrau beer featuring in two influential scenes: recurring role as a transvestite DEA agent and as a narrator in the Showtime erotic TV series Red Shoe Diaries. This was his breakthrough as far as the industry is concerned. It is during this time that he tasted his first commercial success.

His good start enabled him to break to stardom when he played an influential role in the movie "Working girl" which

---

[1] For the record, I worked as a newspaper boy from the age of fifteen.

led him to even a bigger role in the low budget movie by the name "New Year's Day". Still unsatisfied with his achievement, David decided to do things differently. He first fired his agent and switched to Hollywood where the desire to achieve prompted him to hire fresh representative. His 1990's life was low profiled though he played small and quick roles in the film The Rapture, Julia Has Two Lovers and Kalifornia.

The appearances that Duchovny received on popular TV shows gave him the confidence to diversify his ventures. He realized that he could succeed more in TV than in the film. Therefore, inspired by this new finding, he rolled up his sleeve and begun conducting different TV shows which are up-to-date very relevant. And in 1993, his acting carrier was beginning to flourish. He landed a promising role as an FBI agent known as Fox Mulder, on the sci-fi TV series, *The X-Files*. At this stage, David intrigued the audience with the chemistry he portrayed with fellow actor Gillian Anderson. It was hard to tell whether Gillian and David were just co-actors. One can be tempted to believe that there was something going on behind the scenes between David and Gillian. However, he denies all this and maintains that it was all about work and nothing else. I must admit, I totally agree and wouldn't suggest otherwise.[2]

The Golden Globe Award he later received for staging the best TV show was one of the most inspiring awards that catapulted David to stardom for it gave him the much-needed will power to hit the top. His show managed to beat

---

[2] Don't sue me.

all the TV shows to this award in 1995 and in 1998, they decided to venture elsewhere. So they decided to shoot the last movie for the series - *The X-Files*. Still driven by the passion to take a bigger slice out of the industry, David returned to the big screen and immediately embarked on shooting some of the most prolific movies of the time. He shot at least one movie a year, a rate that can only be laughed at by the James Franco's of the world, and in 2007 he made a full time return to TV with his starring role as Hank Moody in HBO's *Californication*.

David made a formal entry into the league of married men in May 6, 1997 when he married actress Tea Leoni whom he had dated for only 3 months. They were blessed with a daughter, Madelaine West Duchovny. They had to wait till 2002 to see their second child, KYD.

Surprisingly, he once confessed to be a sex addict and would seek rehab treatment raising jitters in the family. The result was numerous misunderstandings. This lead to a brief separation. They again separated in 2011 with neither of them non-committal on the divorce issue.

His relationship with the Madelaine is still unknown up to now. However, sources close to him indicate that they still communicate but that cannot be authenticated. I daren't say any more, as I feel I'm only a couple more paragraphs away from a defamation case.

The reason for this short coverage of Duchovny's accomplishments so early on is that it fills up a page. That, and the fact it is highly relevant. Reading Duchovny's biography reads in a way that parallels Hank Moody's fictional life. Moody, like Duchovny, is originally from New York, an East Coast kid, who made the journey west to

Hollywood when he got his break. I'm not too sure how well Duchovny's life mirrors Hank Moody's once he arrived in Los Angeles though and, once again, for fear of being sued by Mr. Duchovny, I can't possibly offer comment on this. I guess Duchovny's portrayal of the character is so uncanny that it would be easy, and naïve, to suggest that this is the case, whereas in fact I'm sure it couldn't be further from the truth. In fact I'm certain David Duchovny is a real good man; more of an Atticus Finch than a Hank Moody.

I digress. Hank Moody is, of course, the central protagonist of the US TV show, *Californication*. He is a successful novelist who is suffering from writers block for a number of hedonistic reasons. He shamelessly lives the bawdy and alcohol fuelled life of a bachelor and he loves it. Oversexed, cocky and charming, his riotous existence provides the basis for the show, but there is more to the character than this. Beneath the lifestyle, Moody finds himself despondent and self-sabotaging at times. Throughout the show, he has consistently been presented as a troubled character and this has developed across each season as he finds himself in bizarre and outrageous situations, often related to his womanising ways.

Originating from the East Coast of America, the erratic Hank Moody moves to LA when his book is optioned to be made into a movie. Following the highs of the success of this book, Moody then finds himself on a downward spiral when the subsequent movie, for which he wrote the screenplay, fails to make the expected impact and he struggles to produce a follow up novel. As a writer, Moody is talented, but tormented. At times he is presented as a poetic and melancholy writer stereotype, but more often than not he can be found at the other end of the spectrum.

Moody will openly embrace the comedy of a tragic situation, always ready to respond with a casual or witty comeback. He has an ego which he uses to his advantage, though this is also what seems to get him in trouble most of the time. He'll use his charms on anyone and everyone and follows a path that generally seems to leave a trail of wreckage along the way. Hank battles with an internal struggle as the different facets of his personality and conflicting desires fight it out to reign triumphant.

Aside from the complexities of his personality, Hank Moody has a love of women, rock music and cars. His signature look is a black t-shirt, with dark jeans and sunglasses - a simple style that never really changes as the show develops. At the beginning of the show Moody is estranged from the mother of his daughter, Becca, and spends the majority of his time drinking, rather than working.

One of the shows constant themes is Moody's inability to say no to sex, drugs and alcohol and the consequences of this as he attempts to remain a good father and role model to his daughter. He responds to his mistakes with yet more mistakes, carouses around LA with woman after woman and finds himself unable to write and build upon his success as an author. Despite his literary talent, he is creatively lost and crumbling under the pressure of his previous accomplishments.

Hank exhibits the signs of someone who is bi-polar. He can swing between self-loathing and negativity, to someone who is loving and spontaneous. He is a continually crass and brutally honest character who will say what he is thinking. The character has earned respect as he is so shamelessly unapologetic for his flaws. He is what he is and his moral compass will point the way it wants to. Additionally, he is entirely non-judgement of others and their own immoral activities, no matter what has taken place. He is a cad, but he genuinely cares about the women he meets. It's never his intention to 'hurt' anyone and he will put a woman's honour before his own every time, even if she doesn't necessarily deserve it.

A good example of this would be in the first season, when Moody sleeps with a young woman named Mia. He learns afterwards that not only is she underage, but she is also the daughter of his ex-partners fiancée. This is a storyline that follows Hank across the seasons as he is plagued by the unwanted attentions of Mia and her subsequent blackmail with the threat of rape for a novel he wrote. Of course, Mia goes on to publish it under her own name. However, despite the actions of the girl, Moody does not respond to this situation with anger. If anything, he finds himself feeling protective of Mia, putting her behaviour down to her being 'mischievous', rather than 'malicious'.

The scandal of this situation highlights how pliable Moody can be in an effort to keep his women protected and himself out of what would be a very damaging mark on his reputation. Though he didn't know how old she was when he met her, he chooses to succumb to her blackmail and give up his next novel as an alternative to defending himself from her threats.

It also shows Moody's reluctance to make smart life decisions. Rather than find a sensible way to get his affairs in order, he continually self-sabotages himself and remains a mess of a human being. Hank is viewed as somewhat of an anti-hero, due to the fact that he isn't exactly a winner, but an accumulator of lessons and life experience. Many people have found this refreshing and relatable in the face of successful TV role models, whose victories and lifestyles are much more difficult to emulate and relate to.

Another interesting point to the character of Hank Moody is that his actions seem to depend on where he is. It has been noted that while in LA he leads an alcohol fuelled, self-gratifying lifestyle which leads him to suffer from long term writers block, when back home in New York, the seasons seem to bring him back down to earth. He finds his inspiration and is able to write once more. The variety of the weather reminds him of the ever-changing world and pushes him to keep going and increase in productivity. The constant heat and brightness of the LA sun seems to numb this part of Moody, trapping him an ongoing cycle of hedonism and mistakes.

Hank Moody is a complex and layered character. Despite signs of loneliness and contradictory desires, ultimately he only ever does exactly what he wants. It could be said that he is missing an important element, a conscience, to guide him as he makes his decisions. Ultimately though, he genuinely does not care what people think of him. He lives his life unapologetically. Hank is a natural womaniser. He is the ultimate ladies man - unique and impulsive. As a writer, he is experienced and understanding of women, great at communicating with them and giving them what they want.

Another aspect of this could be viewed as an admirable quality. Though the LA life is influential on him, he is only reacting to his base desires. He does not fear the judgement of others and is not intimated by social expectations. Throughout his misadventures, Hank always retains his sense of humour and never takes life too seriously, though this could be viewed as both an advantage and a flaw to his personality. Rather than retaining a sensible medium, Moody goes to the extreme with all aspects of his life.

In spite of the excesses of his life, one of the most important facets of Moody's character is the fact that his family comes first. The relationship he has with his daughter is another focal point of the show. It provides an important contrast to the vice-indulging side of Hank. Becca is a crucial part of Moody's life as she is so often the one person to prevent him from completely tipping over the edge. His teenage daughter shares her father's honesty and intelligence and sometimes takes it upon herself to protect him as best she can. As much as he tries however, Moody is aware of his failings as a father, but never gives up on his attempts to finally get it right. His daughter came into his life before he was ready to be a father, so Hank embarked upon parenthood way before he was ready. Moody is loved by his family, though they cannot help but find him frustrating and selfish most of the time.

Parallel to this is his relationship with Becca's mother, Karen. Throughout the series, the pair are consistently on and off as Moody's mistakes continue to come back to haunt him. When the show begins, his actions have already led his former partner to fuck off with another man. Karen is a fairly quiet and mysterious character, but Hank seems to bring out another, more fiery side of her personality. Though he is constantly trying to get back together with her, Karen's frequent rejection tends to send Hank off in the other direction, thereby proving to herself that she made the right decision. In spite of this, Moody is not used to being told no. This proves a constant source of fascination for the character and keeps him returning to her and fighting for her attentions.

Another important person in Hank Moody's life is his agent and best friend, Charlie. The pair have a common interest in their love of women, and despite his own failings and questionable life decisions, Charlie is a fairly constant aspect of Moody's life. Their friendship is important - they understand each other and Charlie will often act as Moody's partner in crime.

Moody has something of an 'love/hate' relationship with many of the shows central characters, specifically himself. Many people can relate to this character, as his shameless qualities seem to reflect certain aspects of modern man in ways that other TV shows seem to reject, instead choosing to turn many of their central male characters into an idealistic (and unrealistic) example of men today. Hank Moody is not a hero. He doesn't have his life in order and he has absolutely nothing at all figured out. He is quick to drown out each mistake with a new one, ambling through his life without aim or any true idea as to where he is supposed to be going.

Despite his often depraved behaviour, it could be said that this is nothing more than a cover for someone who is lonely and vulnerable. Though he is open and honest to others, he is not necessarily as candid with himself and more often than not finds himself entirely unsure of what he wants and where he is going. Overall, Hank Moody is very much a contradiction of himself. He is a womaniser who is desperate for the love of the mother of his child. He is emotionally immature, incapable of taking responsibility and saying no to the vices that he loves. As a writer, he can be a sensitive soul and his intelligence is obvious, however he finds it difficult to avoid being swept along with the decadence that the LA lifestyle offers.

As we get to know his character more, we come to realise that Moody has many different versions of himself. He sleeps around, but still loves Karen unconditionally. He is a caring father, and the intention of bettering himself for Becca is always there, however other parts of him often seem intent on ruining this for him, such as his inability to say no. Still, he has character. He gets away with the things he does because of his confidence, his energy for life and his charm. With this, he gains not only women, but also friends and jobs.

As his life frequently crumbles, he holds it together and rolls with the punches. His life is a constant battle, and despite his faults, we see the redeeming qualities shining through, often with a rollicking positivity. As an audience, we come to hope that perhaps one day he will straighten himself out. Moody is incessant. He never gives up and will follow whatever part of him is instructing his actions to get him what he wants and where he wants to be. Hank Moody thrives on all that is shocking and gratuitous and he'll respond to it with characteristic wit, however cringe worthy. His audience follow and relate to his journey and though it is accepted that he could make better life choices for himself, he wouldn't really be who he is if he did.

3 BECOMING HANK

"I probably won't go down in history, but I will go down on your sister."

We've broken the character of Hank Moody down into little juicy, bitesized segments, now it's time to start putting it all back together. These next few chapters will look at what it is Hank does, and ways we can mimmick that to become someone that loosely resembles the man himself. Make sure you read the warnings at the end though. Seriously.

Work

Hank is a professional writer. That is how he manages to live a life of relative luxury and leisure. You too can become a writer. It's not difficult, just time consuming. Writing is the art of expressing feelings and thoughts. It has transformed the lives of many people including Hank. In fact, there are guys out there are taking advantage of this digital era to make real money by writing and publishing books online. You too can be like them. You don't have to be a magician for you to make big money. Ignore the critics. Writing books is one of the most rewarding careers. Launch your career today and tell your critics that this time you are coming and you mean serious business. You have a dream and that dream is to make money from writing! Well, you bought a fucking book called *Becoming Hank Moody* so I'd think the idea of writing for a living had crossed your mind at some point!

Gone are those dark days where accessing important materials was a nightmare. We are lucky to be living in a digital age of mass communication. Google is your friend. It provides you with the information you need to write your first book, and the porn you need for when it all becomes too much!

Launching your writing career calls for patience and hard work. Nothing comes on a silver spoon. Except heroin. Everything is worked for. Even herion! So, before you start your career, here are some points to take into consideration.

Change your mindset

Writing is an art that requires a dynamic mind. I know many writers who just want to write what they like most. They forget that other areas can really pay. So if you want to be successful when it comes to writing books, don't restrict yourself to that area you only love. Remember when Hank gets commissioned to write a screenplay. What about when he gets offered the job on for writing a blog post and he takes it? Whilst writing what you love is obviously nicer to do, sometimes, even hank had to write for money. With this in mind, begin writing as a business rather than as a creative outlet. Of course, that's not how Hank started, but if you're merely interested in getting the lifestyle of a successful writer like Hank, you're better off selecting a lucrative niche.

A good number of writers are desperately looking for means of earning a living owing to hard economic times as a result of the global economic crisis. However, this does not mean for you to go wild trying everything, including things you have no talent on. Writer may be your name and fiction your game, but do you have the talent? So before commencing your writing career, ask yourself the following questions: Do I have the talent required? Do my stories make meaningful impact? What if I test my work by publishing it or entering into a competitive contest, will it blink? And, this is where an acclaimed professional editor comes in. They will review your work to establish whether it is worth publication.

Remember though, you're fiction may be shit, but you might be an expert in human resources after working in the dull industry for years. Why not take this experience and put it down on paper. You could even write a memoir about why the industry you've come from is fucked! Those types of books always make for good reading. Just make sure, if you're putting your real name to it, you certain you won't be returning to that particular field. Having written, *Why HR Sucks Cock,* you probably won't be first on the shortlist for new hires!

Locating the market is one of the best things you can do in publishing. Firstly, you can subscribe to magazines that publish fiction. Then, make sure that each magazine you find in doctors office and on newsstands online, is scrutinized. In addition, you need to locate appropriate magazines using available databases. Remember to locate theses databases by visiting their websites to get their submission guidelines.

In addition, knowing what the customers want can save you a great deal. Different fiction has different followings. You can decide to dwell on Westerns, science fiction, mystery, and historical, to name a few. But the bottom-line is that you must provide quality and relevant work for your customers. Worm up to this trick and get a hot topic that has generated great interest and try writing on it. This will help you market your book considering the stiff competion out there.

You should be driven by the passion to achieve. You cannot get to this level if you focus on small areas that will only make you a penny. So don't bypass magazines which you think are not publishing your fiction. You might find that such magazines are seeking your good fiction, and this can kick start your career quite easily.

Before you fully establish yourself, consider writing shorter articles for magazines basing them on your favorite topic. This will provide you the perfect platform to get acquainted with the editors in the market.

You could also double your earning potential by editing fiction works for clients, teaching writing, and perhaps conduct workshops for people interested in sharpening their skills in writing. Again, what does Hank do? He takes a job teaching English. Of course, Hank turns this into an opportunity to acquire a serious amount of 'bed time' with some pretty looking females. You could do the same? Maybe.

As a curious writer, always get a copy of a magazine that pays the big bucks. Also, get the guidelines of the best paying magazines. Remember also to stick to the instructions. For example, if you are requested to submit a 1,000-word inspirational fiction, stick to that number. Don't send them more. Not even two words more. Magazine and newspaper writing is very strict when it comes to word counts. The reason for this is simple. You have a space to fill. If you write more, you're work won't fit in the space allocated. If it's really good, you may be lucky and the editor might move it to a larger space. But the chances of this happening are slim. So just stick to the word count. You will be kicking yourself in the nuts if you don't stick to their submission guidelines. In addition, ensure that the manuscript you submit meets the best quality standards. Nobody, including the editor, has time to edit your pile of shit. So embrace professionalism by polishing your submission to create a brand and followers.

Leave alone the critics; you have the potential of making good money out there. If you have the skills and perhaps you are the prolific writer that many fiction readers want, then the chances are that you are on to a winner. So the trick here is to change your ways, have passion, have the right mindset and do one thing at a time. Don't toss what you have written and switch to the next. Complete it first and submit it before commencing the next. Believe in yourself, because in the first instance, nobody else will.

Now that you know all this, don't start reeling off the excuses. Never complain that you can't make money by writing. Use the resources available and you too, like Hank, can swagger with the money you make from fiction.

Traditional publishing versus self publishing

So if you have decided that you are now to become a fiction writer, you have many options. Among the most common ones are these two prevalent traditional publishing and self-publishing models. Hank followed a traditional publishing model, but before you rush into choosing one of them, you must learn the pros and cons associated to each.

Traditional publishing is a form of publishing that focuses on two people - the publisher and the author. In the former, the author has a duty of completing his or her manuscript. He or she will submit the manuscript to the latter (the publishing house). However, submission can be undertaken by a professional agent. The editor of a publishing house then reads it to establish whether it is good for the house. He or she can decide to reject it or publish it. If rejected, the author can take it to another publisher to see if it can be published. On the other hand, if it's approved and subsequently published, it means that all the rights of the book now belong to the publisher. The author is then paid an advance on future loyalties. The publisher then designs and packages the book ready for marketing and finally distribution to the public. It's the model we're familiar with from *Californication* but it's not the only option available.

Unlike traditional publishing where the author is different from the publisher, self-publishing is a different process. When self-publishing, the author becomes the publisher. He takes the role of the publisher and he or she is charged with the responsibility of proofreading the final text, providing the administrative funds for publishing and also the print-ready artwork. In addition, the author markets the book, distributes it, files press releases for it and runs advertisement campaigns for the book. In self-publishing, the number of copies to be made always used to be decided by the author. This posed a serious challenge in the past as the author produced a shit-ton of copies that usually gathered a lot of dust in the garage because the book suffered from a serious lack of marketing. However, gone are those days, thanks to the introduction of Print on Demand (POD) technology where the author only prints only requested copies. Services such as Createspace (owned by Amazon) allow you to setup your book, upload all the content and artwork, and you won't pay them a penny, until it sells. Then, you pay a percentage of the book price to Createspace (Amazon) to cover the costs of printing.

In traditional publishing, the author can do a lot of waiting before a manuscript becomes a book. First, the manuscript it pitched to several publishing houses before it catches one's attention. And, the worst part of it is the fact that most of these big houses take up to six months working through it. However, this only applies to fiction. Other nonfiction publications can be done more quickly.

Unlike traditional publishing, self publishing consumes a lot of resources and the author pays for everything - editing, design, printing, advertising, distribution to get the book to the reader. On the other hand, traditional publishing is a bit friendly when it comes to money. Here, you are paid an advance, depending on your agreement.

Often authors feel despair when an over-zealous editor of a certain publishing house fails to publish his/her works simply because it is too controversial, or it isn't the one they want or even they think it can't sell. However, with self publishing, the author has complete control over his/her work. He chooses the kind of topics to write and publish, target market, design and appearance. It doesn't matter how shit your book is, you can always self-publish it. Unfortunately, this leads to many self-published authors throwing a ton of money at a shit book to market it. It may sell for a short time, then the reviews hit Amazon; *"Worse than living in Iraq", "I'd rather have listened to One Direction", "When I lost my legs, I felt pretty crap. After I read this book, I wanted to kill myself"*. Self-publishing is a wonderful thing.

Now that you know the fundamental differences between the two, it is up to you to choose which one suits your needs. Ask yourself some critical questions. Do you want to play the waiting game that pays big at long last with traditional publishing? Or are you willing to dig deep into your pocket to have a complete control over your manuscript that guarantees quick turn around?

Luckily for customers, you have the opportunity to

choose between the two by keenly weighing between the advantages and disadvantages listed below. So if you aren't sure which between the two you want, pleases consider there pros and cons.

<u>Self-Publishing Pros</u>

- You can make more money (per book) with self publishing as opposed to traditional publishing.
- Self publishing guarantees efficiency and a book is published within a few minutes.
- Greater control as far as cover design and title is concerned.
- You are your own boss, you cannot be told to edit anything out.
- Unlike the traditional publishing, self-publishing guarantees complete ownership of rights.
- You have a chance of printing in small quantities depending on orders.
- You can still get your book on Amazon.

<u>Self-Publishing Cons</u>

- You will witness limited distribution since most chains don't like self-published work.
- You have to foot all the marketing and distribution costs.
- You have to solely depend on yourself. No one will be there to support you (unless you pay them).
- Sales can be challenging for those people who don't already have a public presence.

- Your book is unlikely to get reviews in larger publications as most reviewers don't like reviewing self-published books.

Traditional Publishing Pros

- It is prestigious to sign a contract with traditional publishing house.
- Increased credibility as an expert.
- Your book can easily get to the international market depending on the aggressiveness of your publishing house.
- Your book will get sent to books stores across the world.
- You'll have a press release written by someone that knows what they're doing.
- You may be given the opportunity to speak in public about your book.
- You media exposure is enhanced.
- All the printing costs are met by the publishing house.

Traditional Publishing Cons

- For your book to sell to a publishing house, you need to put together an extensive
- You will make less than a dollar for each book sold. If you're lucky. And this will be deducted from your advance in the first instance.
- It takes a year or so for your book to get printed after acceptance.
- The fact that the editorial and sales staff come

and go can result in your project getting sacked.

- Limited control over your book design-cover and title.
- You can be told edit anything and everything. Even what you oppose to.
- Although you own the copyright, sometimes it cannot exclusive. You can only own it absolutely if your agent negotiated it.

Ultimately, it's up to you. You can decide to choose either of the two. But irrespective of your choice, the bottom line is that you must personally promote your book. Period.

Working From Home

Ultimately, if writing isn't for you but you still want a slice of Hank's life, it's not impossible. We are lucky to be living in a well enabled information world, thanks to the dynamic technology. The advancement in this sector has routed the world to tread forward into the IT-enabled global economy where almost everything is being done via the internet in the global marketplace. What this means is that if your writing career doesn't take off, there are many more options still available to you. Working from home enables you execute a wide variety of jobs. Ultimately, that's what we're aiming for. Not having to wake up at 9am and do the shitty commute. We want a job we can roll out of bed at 3pm and do for a few hours before hitting the town and playing the ladies. Be sure you read that the right way round! Playing the town and hitting the ladies is not a good move. One that Hank would frown upon. Definitely. Some of the jobs you can do in your underwear is data mining, customer relations management and other marketing jobs which can now be completed online due to the increasing internet connectivity around the world. But before we even go there, let us answer the question, "what is outsourcing?"

Outsourcing is the process of contracting with another person or particular company to undertake a specific function. Nowadays, you will find that a company finds it necessary to outsource in one way or the other. Typically, functions that a company outsources are those considered non-core. For example, if a leading communication company wants to increase its efficiency and market itself efficiently to create a bigger customer base, it may opt seek the services of a renowned advertiser. The work of the advertiser will range from drafting marketing plans, designing the company's website, creating engaging and persuasive content, company's reviews. The outside firm that is providing outsourcing services is known as the service provider.

The growing demand of these services has led to the emergence of freelancing sites that offer perfect opportunities for contractors to make a living. Sites such as oDesk.com, elance.com, and iWriter.com are just a few examples of big timers in this area. They all have a common goal - to link contractors with clients. Odesk.com in particular has established itself as the most reliable freelancing site for both contractors and clients owing to its usability.

The introduction of these modern companies has

dynamically changed the whole idea of working from home. They have diversified their services by offering various services into varied fields. Their branches have been spread to cover fields like customer interaction services, medical transcription, data processing, market research, banks, financial institutions, insurance companies, education and shares. These kinds of jobs are posted in leading freelancing sites like oDesk.com.

With oDesk.com, you can work from anywhere in the world and you can still choose to specialize in the area of your choice. Ideally, the most common areas you can bank on include, web designing, web project management, web developing, data entry, desktop application, copywriting, virtual assistance, personal assistance, network administration, technical writing, internet marketing, logo design, technical support, graphic design, recruiting and bookkeeping just to mention a few.

Did you know that you can earn extra income while working from your comfy at home? Sounds like Hank to me! Many opportunities are cropping up due to the increasing demand of content by various international companies. Luckily, the emergence of online companies is acting like a link between potential contractors and employers hence presenting numerous opportunities for freelancers. So if you haven't started yet, then you are missing out on a lot of opportunities.

The following are some of the advantages of working online.

- **Income** - In the recent times, many online businesses have sprung up therefore expanding the opportunities on the internet of making real income. Some of them include affiliate marketing, freelancing and Google ad sense. You can entirely dictate your income since it all depends on your efforts.

- **Time** - Freelancing is a platform that allows you to work at your own time. Unlike the traditional working environment where you must be physically present in the working location, the online platform allows you to choose when to work and where to work from. Therefore, you have plenty of time to attend to your friends and family.

- **Commute** - The world is witnessing rapid population growth especially in urban areas. As a result, cities have become congested making it difficult to reach your destination in time. You will spend a lot of hours practically doing nothing. However, with online jobs, you don't have to worry about this. All you need is your effort.

- **Your own boss** - I guess you have an idea what a terrible boss can do to your day. Miserable of course! All sorts of shouting and pressure are driving most guys from the traditional working setup. With online jobs, you are your own boss.

- **Passion** - Passion has been outlined as one of

the major reasons why people are flocking on the internet to make a living. In most cases, you will find people dedicating much of their time online simply because they came across something they have passion for. They never mind how much they will earn, but rather will want to achieve their dreams.

With freelancing, you have the opportunity of making up to 6-figures in income. Monthly. However, to meet this target calls for your commitment. With these sites, you can do just about anything apart from giving BJ's, although I guess you could always try. You can work as much as you want, whenever you want, and hence providing you with the opportunity of determining your income. So distance yourself from this crazy poverty mentality which is holding you down.

The most successful freelancers out there can tell you that earning money online is real. Most of them agree that setting personal goals is the first step towards succeeding in this area. For example, if you aspire to make $80,000 a year, you must work to earn at least $1,800 a week. So this means you need to up your freelancing game and make a minimum of around $300 per day. However, the big question is: who will pay you all that and what kind of work will guarantee that?

Before you launch your career, you need to know that time is money. This way you will get to charge the right amount that equals the amount of effort spent on that particular project. Some charge 15 cents for a word if they're writing, while others charge for even more. So it is important to evaluate your skills and determine how much your work is worth.

Various freelancing websites exist on the net nowadays. Most of them are free to join. However, as a newbie you may get paid less due to lack of experience (or at least perceived experience on the website). So at first, clients may pay you less and you may consider charging higher rate as you get your reviews up.

Most of these freelancing sites offer both hourly and fixed jobs. Odesk.com in particular, guarantees payment for hourly jobs. So for beginners, it's wise if you can secure hourly contracts. In addition, if the project entails more details, it's important that you consider charging on hourly rates.

All the above underscores my idea; you can make real money online, especially with freelancing. All you need is a computer, a reliable internet connection, and passion. Get yourself out and join the freelancing community in making real income. Go! Go!

4 GETTING THE LIFESTYLE

"You know, it's true what they say about pot. It's very much a gateway drug. And it can be a gateway to some pretty cool things. But it can also lead to poverty, despair, stunted adolescence, man-breasts."

There are hundreds, if not thousands of books available on the subject of creating an 'ideal lifestyle', but not one of them focuses on creating a Hank Moody lifestyle. That is what this section is all about, and whilst many of the ideas that I'll throw in to the mix are borrowed and developed from other authors and thinkers original work, these ideas are all about getting the lifestyle that most closely replicates that of Mr Moody. In case you've forgotten what that is, go back and read the chapter on Hank's lifestyle.

The 4 Hour Workweek: Escape 9-5, Live Anywhere and Join the New Rich by Timothy Ferriss, first published in 2007, is a highly successful self-help book (it has been translated in more than 30 languages and has sold more than million of copies worldwide).

In the book, Ferriss focuses on unique "lifestyle design" and escaping the traditional lifestyle in which people spend long working hours with rare vacations for decades in order to save money and be able to travel and relax after retirement.

Ferriss challenges this plan, arguing that waiting to live and relax after retirement is not the best way to go. He also doesn't advocate saving. What the book focuses on is how to build a new lifestyle, the one in which you can spend weeks and months traveling around the world while having a constant and sustainable income.

To present these ideas and concepts, Ferriss uses the acronym DEAL (Definition, Elimination, Automation and Liberation). These are also the names of the four main chapters in the book.

D for Definition

In this chapter, Ferriss introduces new terms, objectives and rules of what he calls "the new game". This is an introductory chapter that makes the readers familiarize themselves with the common lingo the author will use in the book. Even more than that, this chapter defines key objectives and goals one wishes to achieve.

One of the most important things the author emphasizes is replacing assumptions. For many people in the US, the assumption is that you have to work hard (usually 12+ hours per day) for 30, 50 years so you can enjoy your retirement. The only breaks you can get are weekends and rare, short holidays. This is one of the main assumptions Ferriss questions and replaces.

Ferriss focuses on the new game, that is, a new view of life and desired outcomes. As he points out, people don't want to have a million dollars in the bank – people want a lifestyle that having a million dollars in the bank can give them, such as less working hours or travelling around the world.

In this chapter, Ferriss introduces a concept of the New Rich (NR) and explains how they operate. The New Rich are people who know how to play the new game to their advantage. These people are not born into wealth and they don't work long hours to earn their money. The NR know how to be the most effective and productive. Another characteristic of the New Rich, points Ferriss, is that they understand the importance of "mini-retirements" throughout life instead of waiting until retirement.

Ferriss also explains the concept of eustress, healthy, positive stress he claims all people need. According to him, the opposite of happiness is not unhappiness but boredom: human beings need a certain dose of excitement in their life.

E for Elimination

In this chapter, Ferriss explains several techniques and concepts intended to eliminate all the unnecessary work. This is particularly important when it comes to time. According to Ferriss, most people waste too much time on unimportant tasks that don't bring money or results. He argues that truly important things take less time than it's believed they do, so the time saved in the process becomes free time.

Ferriss makes a clear distinction between efficiency and effectiveness, and he claims effectiveness should be the goal.

To achieve this, Ferriss introduces two key concepts:

- **The "Pareto Principle",** also known as "80-20" Rule. It says that 80% of your benefits come from 20% of your efforts. Ferriss advises to recognize efforts which actually bring these results and benefits and focus on them while eliminating the rest that doesn't bring much benefit but takes a lot of time.

- **Parkinson's law.** According to this concept, "work expands so as to fill the time available for its competition". Simply put, if you have 24 hours to complete a task it will seem less huge than if you have three weeks to complete it. Shorter deadlines put you into action and make you focus on the actual performance. The more time there is for a task to be completed the more chances that a person will waste time on things like preparation or even obsessing about the project. By using Parkinson's law and short deadlines it is possible to limit the amount of time that is spent working.

In short, this chapter is about learning to ignore the unimportant and focus on what truly brings results. Using these techniques, promises Ferriss, it's possible to achieve better results (and better earnings) in much less time. Ferriss explains how to organize your emails so you will have to check them only occasionally (such as twice per day or even less – Ferriss himself only checks business emails once per week). He also gives tips on organizing phone calls and meetings.

A for Automation

In this chapter, Ferriss teaches principles and techniques of automating your life, namely, putting the cash flow on autopilot. In this chapter the author shows how the income is generated and what you can do to make this system work for you. The goal is to own a business but to eliminate your presence from it. Everything that can be automated should be automated and transferred to other people. This way, the actual work a person needs to perform takes only a little time, which leaves plenty of free time for traveling (or other activities a person wants to do).

To achieve this, Ferriss recommends techniques such as drop shipping: never keep your product in stock but transfer customer orders, shipment, etc. to the manufacturer or a wholesaler. This way, they are the ones dealing directly with the customer, which eliminates a lot of work for the business owner.

Another technique Ferriss recommends is outsourcing your work and tasks to virtual assistants. He particularly recommends overseas assistants: their work generally costs less per hour and another advantage is the time difference. If you live in the US you can assign a task to a virtual assistant in India or China in the afternoon and have it done during night, so it's ready for you in the following morning. This way, argues Ferriss, it's possible to outsource a great deal of the work or just about any task you don't wish to do, such as paying bills.

This chapter also discusses various ways to test products and find out what works the best. Ferriss also talks about using services such as Google AdWords and AdSense to your advantage.

In short, this chapter shows some of the methods and techniques needed to build a sustainable and automatic source of income.

L for Liberation

In the final chapter, Ferriss talks about traveling and mobility. Here, he presents some ideas on what you can do once you automate your life and organize the work the way discussed in previous chapters. In this chapter, Ferriss shows how it's possible to liberate yourself from a geographical location and traditional job.

Ferriss introduces the concept of "mini-retirements", that is, a necessity to take a break between works. He mainly discusses dedicating this free time to traveling and visiting various locations, but the exact way a person wants to spend this time is individual.

According to Ferriss, too much work without rest or enjoyment is not the best solution. Breaks, traveling and these "mini-retirements" are necessary for anybody who wants to be truly productive.

How to live like a Rockstar on a Budget

Ultimately, you want to live like Hank Moody without budgetry constraints. But when you first step out onto the path of Moody, you may not have the luxury of regular royalty payments. This section is for you. Financial management is one of those areas that are proving to be very tricky if not dealt with carefully. It poses great challenges especially to upcoming rock-stars who must quench numerous financial thirsts around them. At some point, if you are a star, you may find yourself incurring not only great loses if you own a business but also become bankrupt. Not because you don't make enough, but for reasons associated with bad financial habits. This can plunge you into bankruptcy thus stabbing your personal image as well as affecting your self-esteem. And, I am sure you will not what this to happen to you. Not now, not even in the near future. So if you have been a worried star when it comes to financial management, we have good news for you. Gone are the days when you used to blow all your cash in fancy holidays, parties, etc. So, if financial freedom is your ultimate goal, keep reading. You are at the right place.

Right off the bat, I believe in being frugal. Successful rock-stars who have made big strides in life can tell you that extravagant spending is for the misguided people .For example, if you are a Hollywood star, spending nights in floors, in bus shelters, in abandoned apartments is not an embarrassment. In fact, this may be a big plus in your career for it may be a budge of honor. For most guys, they will rather spend that boring life simply because they don't want to be associated with this kind of life they consider low-class. Many may not approve this but the truth of the matter is that this is more than staging that stunning TV show. And, rock-star magicians know what this means. They will tell you that people of this kind don't do things according to their own mind. They are missing out on big fun out there by restricting themselves to this dull lifestyle.

Due to the sensitivity of this matter, I have decided to focus on some of the key tools you can use to achieve great success for your career and financial life as a whole. Don't live in the past and yet you have better prospect than you'd think. In fact, you are a step away from a bright and promising life if you follow my steps.

Financial management, like any other sensitive issue in life, is tricky and you need to be careful not to squander all you have built all these years. Just as you cannot rock the house without having the right equipment, you cannot also prosper unless you have the right financial programs.

Financial programs focus mainly in tracking one's spending. Over the years, programs have been invented to assist people in managing their cash more efficiently. However, this does not mean that you go cutting your budget even for the basic wants. No. Financial programs say otherwise. They are specifically targeted at letting people understand that before you spend what you have, evaluate where your money is and where it goes or your necessary expenditure.

Logically, if you become aware of your cash flows, you will get to magically manage it. Think of any managing software in the market, they are all designed to make you manage your finances more smoothly and effectively. Experience tells me that if you use all these financial programs well, you will make tremendous financial management strides-a key step in achieving your financial goals. This is one of the most effective ways in achieving financial freedoms. They are the most reliable keys towards financial sanity. Try them today.

Various programs can be found from online vendors. It is up to you to make an informed decision on the program you will like to use. But before choosing make sure you evaluate your needs so that you can choose the one that suits your needs.

Staying on top of the game as far as financial management is concerned can be challenging. Even the big rock stars who have managed to stay on top can tell you that it's really hard to stay up there. But for sure they will tell you that their biggest gains have been made as a result of having plans which they strictly follow. You too can be like them if you map out a financial plan and start following it. Believe them. They are some of the simplest ways of welcoming financial success to your life.

Nowadays we have numerous financial planning tools available online. They are designed to let everyone use them in a bid to enable you organize your financial needs more efficiently. They will give you a good sense of what you should do in order to reach your goals. All you have to do is to surf through the net to find some of them to achieve your financial freedom.

Research has shown that friends can influence one's behavior including spending habits. And, if this research is anything to go by, you need to choose your pals carefully. You don't have to keep friends just for the sake of having them. Choose somebody who will contribute positively in your life and shake off the bad ones out.

In addition, you can decide to be around this upbeat guy you dream as your mentor. But be sure to control your finances. This is because they at one time can mislead you into spending your money lavishly. Most of them will love to "ride the wave of enthusiasm". They are the veteran in this game. They are the movers and shakers and you are the learner. Don't get carried away. Be sure to control important aspects of your career for a better financial freedom

Any big star must know the direction his/her life is taking. You too must evaluate yourself and see if you are going forward. Are you good savings enough? Are you making the right investment? Is your business progressing? Try to establish some of the greatest success ingredients and try to duplicate them. You will definitely succeed especially if you put this into practice and manage your time properly. So what are the ingredient sauces for success?

Your financial success can only say yes to your life if only you plan yourself. If for example your life isn't getting to the desired direction try to learn lessons from the past. Try to establish that part that isn't on the right track. Doing the same thing that's not registering any recommendable change or progress is a classical definition of insanity. Just try to learn lessons from the past and get to the root cause of the problem. However, if you don't establish it, don't worry because the next point will be of great assistance.

Hiring a coach is one noble idea one needs to do. You should hire a financial coach just like every winning artist will hire a coach. You can identify individuals who have really made it in this area of specialization and ask them to be your mentor. By so doing, you will surely see off your career heading to untold success.

Teachers and coaches are the people with great financial experience. You will have to go to them with your ideas and some details concerning your spending preferences, estimated income and some additional details they may require. However, the good news is you only need to report to them at least once every month. They will then give their feedback and suggest areas you will need to polish.

Being an artist can be very challenging. People expect so much from you. You need to use your resources carefully by balancing between your career and the society. You will not want your society to view you as the selfish guy simply because you ignore them or you don't positively participate in important activities. So go for a holiday once a year and dedicate some of your time in visiting the needy. It will be so amazing if you give surprise visits to your local hospital with foodstuffs, toys, gift cards and perhaps clothing. This will at least put a smile in the faces of struggling, sad and lonely parents. Be selfless and for sure this self indulgent idea will bring happiness to the sick. You can also take your kids with you.

Volunteering is one's inner calling. Involving yourself in such activities like cleaning your town and planting trees can blend your career and financial life with your image. It can be it at Homeless Shelter, animal Hospital. Just follow your passion. Just donate anything and you would have made a tremendous difference in somebody's life. You can volunteer at the hospital where many sick babies need such attention. Just do something. Go and do something! Did you know that there are many people in need of blood? It will be very noble if you save a life by donating blood and platelets? According to statistics, the demand for blood is growing as the world population hits its record high. And, saving one's life just takes a bold step of donating blood. It isn't hard. All you need to do is to register as a bone marrow donor. That's it, that's all!

Involving yourself in cancer campaigns is better than selling a platinum album in my opinion. You can earn a real reputation and live like a rock-star in society if you spare some of your resources and few dollars. It will be unwise for you to make billions and yet somebody out there is suffering because he/she cannot afford the medication fee.

As a celebrity you are in a better position to be listened to than any ordinary person. Be it the president, your favorite and powerful, media station, favorite celebrity, congress, small and big companies, NGOs, schools, universities and all academic organizations. Shout until people hear you. At the end of the day you will be the hero and your music or art will easily sell for simple reason-you always give back to the society.

Alternatively, you can also use hook-ups in the society to get your message across. Hook-ups will enable you travel all over the world in the name of cancer campaigns. You will virtually end up spending nothing. In fact, you will find yourself living frugally by returning home with few dollars out of donations from corporate world.

This can be done by making hook-ups with people by offering them your friendship and value. This may be ordinary cancer campaigns, but guess what....your sales will never hit ground zero again.

Being a celebrity is somewhat misinterpreted and most people think that it means trashing hotel rooms plus waking up at 3 p.m. to start daily activities. However, the point is that it goes beyond this. In fact, it is somewhat the opposite of this. The staggering truth is to have financial freedom by taking real advantage of the tools in this article.

All the above underscore my idea-living like a rock star calls for great sacrifice and dedication as well as being disciplined. You must understand that being living like a rock-star is more about image than reality. This means that if you want to register the best image, you will need to implement all these simple ideas. This will enable you lead a sour financial life. Get out of debt, invest responsibly and effectively. Control your financial life. And, you will obviously benefit by feeling like a rock-star. Take your financial life and turn it around for the best. And, that is a classical definition of what a real rock-star is!

So, are you going to be a rock-star? Don't let anything stand your way! Be one today, no tomorrow excuses!

5 STYLE, STYLE, STYLE

"That is a prime example of what's wrong with the younger generation today – you leave nothing to the imagination."

The epitome of the cool father, Hank's style is effortless, yet strangely difficult to achieve. His looks score him some major points of the attractive male scale, to the point where I find myself erect whilst watching occasionally. The reason? His style.

What do you think of when you hear the word 'style'?[3] The clothing you wear? The way somebody walks? It has to be one of the most widely used terms, that everybody

---

[3] As in, "His style is awesome", rather than, "That necklace is stylish".

understands, but when it comes to defining it (like now), the mind goes blank. Many would describe it as just a sum of what you are wearing, but I believe it goes deeper than that, past the outer-clothing, past the skin, right to the core of our beings. My reasoning for such outlandish claims; go and wear some clothing that have just come off the catwalk[4] and you'll soon realise you look like an idiot in them, despite the fact they looked so 'stylish' on the model. It's the same when you try on a friends jacket. It sometimes just doesn't feel right, and you end up walking round with your arms jutted out like you're nailed to a cross.

On top of that, how many times have you heard somebody say something and wondered how they got away with it. The Scottish comedian, Frankie Boyle, tells some jokes which I daren't even write here for fear of being beheaded by some minority activist group, yet because that is his 'style', he can get away with it. I guess the best way to describe the word 'style' to an alien then, would be to just substitute the word for 'expression'.

Style is the product of you. The way you dress. The work you do. The way you talk. All of that helps to make your style – and whether you think you're 'stylish' or not, you'll be pleased to know that you still have style. It's yours, and nobody else can touch it. That's not to say that it must remain the same for the indefinite future. Style is something that can be changed, altered. Change your clothes, and you've just transformed your style. It's the same with your haircut. You can be even more drastic and change your job, car, or even where you live, and this will all rework your style, for better or worse.

---

[4] Runway for my American friends.

Taking a more in-depth look at the word, style is a broad word and it takes various meanings. In most cases, the word is used to refer to the way you dress, talk, and move your body. Factually, the term style can also to refer to the way you express your inner thoughts or being, outwardly. In addition, it is worth noting that whatever you express outside reflects your inside. It may be seen through your feelings, thoughts, interests, and values.

Style is not just the outer appearance. Many people think that style is just about good looks and perhaps great outfit. This is the reason you will find many people trying to look for a style coach, hoping that their outer appearance, especially the clothes, is improved. It is true that a stylist is very important as far as your style is concerned as they will ensure that the clothes suit you and your figure. Their job is to pinpoint the areas you ought to improve to accomplish your target style.

However, besides your outer appearance, you must take time in shaping your communication skills for they are critical is style building. Communication supplements your outer image. Some people talk quietly and succinctly, whilst others, like Hank, are a bit more outspoken. That's not to say they just blurt out the first thing that comes to mind, but they certainly deliver the message in a slightly different way.

Sometimes people talk carelessly and fail to adopt the best way to put a point across. And, the result is discontent from your audience. To prevent this from further embarrassing you, you need your style coach to pinpoint all your weak point and perhaps suggest better way of going about your style.

Reputation is one of the key ingredients of style. You need to be bold. Also, brand yourself positively for this will influence the way people view you. Don't allow someone to taint your reputation since this is likely to negatively impact on your general style. It is hard to change a tainted reputation.

Psychologically, reputation is associated with self-esteem. This has a great bearing on the way you think and perhaps the way you relate with others. For example, you are introduced in a public rally as the founder of a local NGO that has transformed the lives of many. People will attentively listen to what you have to say and they will definitely trust your words as opposed to this guy introduced as a local shop-worker.

So how do we fix your style? Well, going full circle, kick-starting the impression you register in people's mind depends on the clothes you wear. Research has shown that clothes people wear carry special 'message'. This may be the reason we have different clothes for different functions. So if you want to make a perfect style out of yourself, take time in choosing your clothes wisely. Hank almost has a uniform. His reasoning for this would perhaps be because of his late night rendezvous with women, but also perhaps because it is easier. Hank doesn't like to complicate matters that don't need complicating. Perhaps you could learn from this and develop your own uniform for different occasions?

For every occasion you attend, ensure that the clothes you wear carry the same message as the occasion itself. Be smart so that people can see a resourceful guy in you. Don't dress shaggy or dirty simply because you are in a hurry.

People won't take you seriously. Take for example two guys claiming to be managers. The first guy is dressed elegantly and his attire features a well fitted suit. The second guy is dressed in this ill-fitting dirty shirt with no tie. Will people believe him?

Did you know that grooming forms part of your outer image? Now you know, and you need to pay extra attention as far as your grooming is concerned if you want people to judge you positively. People tend to associate general body grooming with personality. Therefore, any style coach will always stress on your grooming whenever you meet people.

For example, imaging Hank giving a lecture on the importance of self discipline to some students at his local university. Yes, Hank is learned and holds an influential position, but the message that is being delivered via his general grooming will dilute the intended message. That, and the fact he hasn't got a clue about self-discipline. Good grooming has been identified as the first step towards self-confidence. When you are dressed well with tidy hair, people will view you as the resourceful person in society. And, everything you say is taken seriously.

Hank is a free spirit and he has this attitude of taking no-shit-from anyone. His communication is an important aspect of his style. The way it is conveyed carries many meanings. This is why if you greet someone "How is your day?" and that person casually responds "Cool" with a frown and crossed arms, you will know that the person isn't really as fine as he claims.

This shows that the message that we get across people does not solely depend on the wordings. It is a combination of many aspects among them body language. In fact, it carries more meaning than any other form of communication.

Also, tone, pitch, and volume of our voice constitutes to nonverbal communication; an important aspect of style. The way we use them can be interpreted differently. For example, someone who likes talking with a loud voice is considered insensitive and egotistical. In other cases, a public speaker may opt speak loudly before a noisy audience in order to catch their attention. On the other hand, soft-spoken guys are considered shy and insecure. They are not brave enough to address people. They think that what they have to say has no meaning. It all depends on the situation and your audience. If you stick to one style throughout life, be ready for some falls.

You probably want to attain the best style that will enable you become the person you want to be. Therefore, you need to model your character towards achieving your dreams. In that case you must understand why you need all the above in full.

Having vision in life can be termed as a personal responsibility. And, if you find a mismatch of whatever kind to your vision, then understand that it is normal and you have a chance of growing because nobody was born perfect. So the closer you are to your ideal vision, the better for you. This is the first step towards fulfilling your dreams.

Also, happiness has been associated with self-esteem. This means that you will get to like yourself more if you are happy. You will get to believe in yourself, and this is the "real style."

So if you have been dreaming to become that person you see in your dreams, the secret is simple: continue working on yourself until you reach your destination.

Self actualization comes hand in hand with self enhancement. Action is needed if you are to achieve the target. And, the only person who can initiate that change is you. You must understand that action does not come by accident. You must induce it.

Film and take pictures of yourself on a regular basis

Do you remember the last time you watched yourself in a film? Filming helps in evaluating yourself. In addition, it helps you in identifying key weak area and focus on how to improve. With such films and pictures, you can monitor your posture, tone, general body appearance, self expressions, and the way you talk. So make a folder of your current pictures and don't forget to get a friend film you. This will give you tones of self-awareness: the first step towards self enhancement as far as the style is concerned.

Send the pictures to your trusted friends

Request them to evaluate them. Let them suggest if the guy in question looks successful, intelligent and attractive. They will definitely send feedback to you. Work on the weakest point and if possible try to improve every aspect of your life with the notes from them. Check whether the notes from your friends are really in line with your target.

Now that you know where you are, make a choice on your next moves. Ask yourself what kind of a person you want to be. Then, gear your efforts towards that direction.

Be assured that result will be worth the effort!

Hire a coach

A good coach will ensure that the route you want to take is the right one. His/her work is to pinpoint the areas you ought to improve as you seek to get the style you want. A coach can either be a sports coach, body building. But all of them have a common goal: making you better that you were when you came.

Choose your friends wisely

Friends can influence the way you think, do things and relate to others. Do not just choose friends for the sake of it. Take time and reevaluate them. Weed the bad ones out for they will damage the image you have worked for this long. You will rather have no friends than have those who will lead you to hell. Be honest. Make the right choice.

In addition, you can also decide to choose your friends from varied sources. For example, you can choose your friends from celebrities, books, tapes and videos.

Change your habits

Habits can harm your style for they can damage one's reputation. Even if you concealed your bad habits, they will at one time damage your image. So the only way to build a good reputation is by changing your habits. This can take a while, but the results are worth it.

Be the patient guy

Change doesn't come overnight. It will take some time to realize positive changes in your life. Also, you can't expect people to appreciate changes in your life within a day! It has taken you long to be where you are. Similarly, it will take you sometime to land where you want to be. Never rush, just keep on working on the weak points. Change is a journey.

Adjust your appearance

Change doesn't come by accident. So work towards becoming the guy you want to be. This does not mean that you imitate other people. Try to be natural. If possible re-brand yourself with unique outfits, good grooming and general body appearance. This will project you as the responsible guy before your acquaintances. And, if you do not know how to do this, get a qualified style coach from either online or a town near you. Don't just stop at your clothes though. As style is a sum of everything you do, take a look at other things that epitomize you. Hank, for example, has a love for smoking, having sex, and drinking. However, he has some few pieces he never takes for granted and helps us to define his style; his typewriter and his Porsche.

His Porsche is a unique car and he loved it especially because of its individuality. The seats in particular are 'covered in pussy juice'. To be exact, the car can be described as rough and damaged, just like the owner. People say that you can look like your dog after long time together and I am beginning to see this in Hank with his car. In fact, some striking similarities and differences between him and his car can be seen. Look at the colours. He loves black jeans and black t-shirt and wears a pair of boots complimented with some exotic sunglasses. His car, a

1990 Porsche 911 Carrera Cabrio [964] looked black. It has embraced the dull and grey colour which now looks broken. This gives a wider picture of immense amount of character as that of Hank.

The Porsche 964 was a great car of its time and it used to perform much like Hank. Now though, it's beginning to fall apart, similarly to Hank himself.

All the above underscores my idea: style defines Hank more than anything.

Improve your style of speaking

Communication is a fundamental aspect that influences the way people perceive you. So when communicating with people, make sure you use good language. And, by good language I mean that you should get rid of blue words and embrace words that are socially accepted. Work on your vocabulary and go an extra mile by working on your diction and accent. This will ensure that people don't judge you based on the speech.

The bottom line

Style development and personal development are two parallel aspects in human beings. The former focuses on shaping your for the world to see you, while the latter is more of yourself. In addition, it is important to note that style development focuses on making you relate with others in a modest way. So getting yourself to learn and develop more in the areas of fashion, body language, and social skills has a striking impact on the way you relate with friends, coworkers, and opposite sex friends. So take your bold step today. Re-brand yourself for a better tomorrow!

6 BUILDING THE CONFIDENCE

"Girls know at once whether they want to fuck, marry, or kill a guy. Which begs the question: how am I doing?"

Hank is a confident person. If you want to be like Hank, you'll have to build your confidence. If you've got none at the moment, don't worry. If you do have some confidence, you'll need more! It can be very tough to build your confidence if you are a naturally inhibited and shy person. Everyone wants to be confident. We admire those who seem totally self-assured and at peace with their lives, and often wish that we could emulate this success. There are always moments that we allow to slip by due to our shy nature or low self-esteem; moments when we should have spoken up when we had something to say. Building your confidence is not instantaneous and there are often a lot of complicated emotional processes to go through before you get there.

Firstly, you have to acknowledge and answer to your insecurities. Everyone has these nipping away at their mind, and though they can sometimes be ignored, you know that at some point they will return. It is likely that these little niggles will never truly go away. It could be something about your personal appearance that you do not like, or perhaps something in your personality that you would like to change. It could be the way you view other people - maybe you find it hard to trust due to a bad experience in the past? Either way, we all have things that bother us and prevent us from feeling confident at times, but it's important not to let our insecurities keep us down. There are many things that you can do to try and improve how you feel about yourself and how you come across to the rest of the world.

A great way to begin dealing with your anxieties is to write each one down. Writing is a wonderful therapy, and it really does help if you allow yourself a pen and paper to process any insecure thoughts. In doing this, you are able to physically see your thoughts in front of you and this will enable you to analyse and give order to what is in your head. What is the problem? What is the reason for the problem? How can you fix it? It's amazing how differently you will see things once you write everything down - sort of like unravelling the knots! Rather than wasting time worrying about these things and going round and round in your head, make the decision to take some control and really deal with it.

Most of the time, we focus on the negative aspects of ourselves, so for once pay some attention to the good parts. What do you like about yourself? What have you achieved in your life that you are proud of? What great experiences have you had? We are quick to judge our faults, but not so quick to praise ourselves. This is one of the key aspects of confidence - a positive and happy outlook, so going forward try not to be so down on yourself! You'll feel better and other people will naturally take notice of your optimistic personality. Think about it - everyone appreciates being around someone who is happy and confident. Take something away from that and try to be that person yourself.

Another important piece of advice is not to make yourself into a victim. You should definitely talk to family and friends about serious concerns, and accept their help and advice, but also take responsibility for yourself. Issues and traumatic events can stick with us for years and really wear us down, leaving us inhibited and introverted. Some things have to be processed and understood, and the avoidance of this can really break your confidence.

If you know you have an unresolved issue in your head, then perhaps it is time to analyse, understand and accept it so that you can begin to heal and move on with your life. Take your lesson from it and leave it in the past where it belongs. Of course, some things just aren't that easy, but even the smallest attempt at fighting your demons can make a huge difference to how you feel about yourself. Think of your mistakes as learning experiences. Everything that we do goes towards shaping us into who we are and who we will become.

Once you feel like you may be on the right track, begin to visualise who you would like to be in the future. You could even try writing it down. If you are looking to build your self confidence, then it is likely you are imagining yourself as someone who is happy, secure and thriving, great at meeting new people and making small talk, and someone who generally knows how to succeed in every situation. The big life changes that we want to make don't always come easy. Often we find ourselves facing large obstacles, so backing down and giving in usually seems like the less troublesome option. Try taking this option away. Don't give up and be incessant. We really do have to work for the things we want, and though it's tough not to shy away, draw on your inner strength to keep you going.

Change what you can change. If you are unhappy with your appearance, then put the work in to fix this. If you want to exercise and have a fitter body, then you have to put the effort it to get what you want. Of course it is difficult, but think how wonderful you will feel once you start to see some results! If you are insecure about your physical appearance, then change it. Give yourself a fresh new look and clothes. If it's your home habits, or constant procrastination that's keeping you down, try a to-do list and stick to it! Keep a tidy house and stay on top of your responsibilities. Reward yourself with TV at the end of the night, rather than as soon as you get home. The little changes can often be the catalyst for the bigger ones. Get your life in order with small steps, and then start to think about the larger tasks which lie ahead.

Pursue some hobbies and be sociable. It's not always easy at times. Often we just want to stay at home and shy away from the effort of putting ourselves out there and getting to know new people. You will find though that once you pick up a hobby you enjoy, you will feel more confident and happy. There are so many different types of hobbies, sports and pastimes out there, and countless social groups for every kind of person, so you really can't fail to find somewhere you will fit in. It's hard to make a go of these things sometimes, but you will find that most of the people out there are just like you - looking to build their confidence and be more sociable. Add some strings to your bow and enhance your uniqueness. You will feel like a more productive and complete person, as well as increasing your chances of meeting people with similar interests.

Make a decision right now to live your life with a bit more pride and grace. Accept compliments, smile and be friendly and none judgemental. We often hide our own insecurities with a bad attitude towards the people around us and it doesn't make you the sort of person that others will think kindly of. Build up your principles and sense of decency. Make effort with your family and friends. When you are at work, really work and put your all into what you are doing. Do a good deed for a stranger. Be interested in other people, offer compliments and help them if you think they need it. Little things like this can often make a person's day, and you will come away with a small sense of pride in yourself. Be a positive force in a world full of negativity.

Something that many of us do is become completely submerged in who we are and what other people are thinking of us, and this can really affect your confidence.

Being self-aware is important, but remember that there is a line between being self-aware and being self-involved. If you are low in confidence, then you may be very conscious of how you come across in any given situation. You'll be wondering what other people thought of you, what you looked like, or if you said or did the right thing. You may spread these concerns to other people, as you require their assurance, but it's not the correct way to improve your self-esteem. Though the approval of others will give you a temporary boost in confidence, this will lead you to continually seek reassurance from those who shouldn't necessarily have to give it to you. It's not their responsibility to put your mind at rest. Often people aren't paying us anywhere near the amount of attention we are imagining in our heads and it's important to remember this. Be fearless as you go about your everyday life and stop worrying what others are thinking.

Take some time to consider how you view other people, particularly the ones you admire. Often these are caring, graceful people who tend to give a lot of their time and thoughts to others. As an exercise, try to emulate this. Try not to draw the focus back to yourself and the insecurities you may have, and instead focus on whatever subject is at hand. Give your attentions to something or someone else. Make a valuable contribution to a conversation. Be kind to people and offer praise to those who have earned it. Present yourself as someone who isn't constantly worried about how they are coming across to the world. It's a heavy weight to carry around with you, so try and shed these concerns and you will naturally become more carefree.

Something else that can effect a person's confidence is the way we are constantly comparing ourselves to other people - their personality, what they look like, the places they go and the things they have achieved. It's such a natural aspect of everyday life that often we don't even notice we are doing it! Most of the time though, we like to present the very best parts of ourselves to the world. We don't want people to see our faults, so remember that next time you are comparing yourself to someone who always seems totally put together. Keep in mind that they too will have insecurities and issues. Everyone is different. We look different, learn and think different and view the world different! We are all unique. That's not to say don't take inspiration from those whom we admire. It's a wonderful thing to learn from others and take their advice, but make it your own and embrace your individuality.

An extension of this thinking is to consider your values and beliefs. Are you someone who just follows along with what other people think, even if it's not necessarily what you agree with? This isn't the way to build self-confidence. Do what you believe in, and fight for that in the face of adversity. You will instil a sense of pride in yourself, and even if others don't always agree, you will gain the respect of people for being someone who sticks to their guns.

Keep in mind that being confident is an important balancing act. People with low confidence may not feel good about themselves, and will often have lots of things they want to change in their life. On the other end of the spectrum however, there are those who are too confident, and often come across as arrogant and uncaring. You need to find a happy medium between the two; one that you are happy with and can build upon.

Give yourself pep talks. If you feel yourself slipping, then think about the things you are grateful for in your life. If you continually beat yourself down with negative thoughts about yourself, then you will only slip lower and lower. Rise above this sort of thinking and keep at it until it feels natural. Be happy with how you look and feel. Put the work in until you get to where you want to be, and remember to do it with patience and positivity! Continue to picture yourself as the person you want to be and put the work in until you get there. It's a long road, so lighten your load, begin with small steps, and start your journey.

7 ATTRACTING WOMEN

*"If I can make you laugh like that, why can't we be together?
That's what I don't understand."*

Hank is a man who gets women. If you want to become someone that loosely resembles Mr Moody, you'll need to learn how to bed yourself some women. Of course, you could equally turn into the homosexual version of Mr Moody. That would be pretty fucking cool. So I guess with that in mind, here is how to attract the sex you are interested in. Or even the sexes. Bi-Moody is cool too.

I know of many men who are suffering in silence and yet they have the solutions with themselves. I understand how tricky it may be to approach a someone especially if you are a newbie. You may have tried numerous tricks (sending flowers, gifts and poems) without any progress. But hey, there is one thing you haven't done. So before you blame your whole looks and perhaps giving up on women, ask yourself if you have really utilized some of the best tricks/tips of attracting women am going to lay down in this article. This section tries to explore some of the most proven tips of attracting women. So if you are single and you want them to flock your way without splashing the cash as most men do, then this is the place for you. Keep reading!

First off, keep your body clean. Women love guys who know how to keep themselves tidy, smart and clean. Go out there and ask any girl if she will want to date a guy who doesn't take regular showers. Just know that women will not want to deal with your week-old BO. So men, take regular showers and style up by using deodorant. The results will be amazing and girls will flock your way.

Secondly, dress nicely like a responsible guy. We mentioned this in the style section, but it's worth covering off again with some more actionable advice. It is an important aspect that plays an important role in attracting people. Try to wear rags and then approach that dream girl of yours, you will be surprised. Ladies (and men) value the way you look; and the way you look is much influenced by the clothes you wear. Just wear clothes that fit you well and which portray you as a responsible guy. You must understand that no woman will want to be embarrassed before her friends simply because you are dressed shaggily. Choose your brand careful by going shopping online for decent clothes. This will get them closer to you than ever.

How about smelling amazing too! I know that every man will love it when his girl (or guy) smells like a princess (or prince). Likewise, women too love men who smell nicely. You can achieve this by keeping your body clean by taking regular showers using nice deodorants, and then wearing nice clothes. You can blend that by adding some modern aftershave and she will love it. If you're not doing this already, you seriously need to buck the fuck up. Smell good, and the BJ offers will be numerous!

I remember one time I was having a casual conversation with a friend about the kind of a woman he was looking forward to meet. I was surprised that he preferred a fairly skinny girl. He went on to point out that such ladies are considered decent, beautiful and perhaps healthy. So, in general, body fitness was top on his list. Therefore, just as you as a man may prefer ladies of this kind, ladies too (generally) prefer decently fit guys. Don't get me wrong. I am not saying that you try to look like the Arnold Schwarzenegger we know, no. What I mean is that you need to stay healthy. You can visit the gym for some body building, devise good diet for yourself, and perhaps try to stay stress free. Your skin will look amazing and the result will be good looks.

In general, most online health blogs are specifically targeted at safeguarding your general body health by providing useful healthy tips such as healthy eating habits and workouts. Therefore, if you want to take your body health to the next level, visit these health blogs. They are very helpful as far as your health is concerned. Stop blaming anybody or anything…the choice is yours!

Research has shown that most ladies love men who do things in a cool and unique way. Think of exploring talents such as playing guitar, musical instrument and singing. Ladies love such men for they represent responsible and exciting partner to meet. So if you are out there wondering on how to keep these ladies attracted to you, here is a loophole; exploit your talent. However, if you feel that you don't have any talent, don't worry. You can try to learn activities such as drawing for they are better learnt than others. In addition, try hanging out with friends whom you think have great talent.

Don't be the guy who sits home all weekend just eating and playing COD. You are locking yourself from the excitements out there. Think of great fun you are missing by choosing the boring life at home. Be it hiking, hanging out with friends, going for a night club, video show etc. But the point here is to keep your life exciting by meeting amazing people!

But get me right, I am not condemning introverted guys, no. All I am saying is that you need to go an extra mile in becoming the exciting guy women want. Remember, you will not meet these ladies if you just stay indoors watching or sleeping all the weekend. Watching won't bring her to you. Go out there and hang out with friends, make new friends and have fun. This is the classical definition of what an "exciting guy" is.

Did you know that having a negative attitude can harm your relationship with your friends? Research has shown that guys with negative attitude usually develop poor relationship with people. Imagine this well-dressed, healthy, financially stable, good looking guy walking along the streets kicking people's property, punching kittens and has this negative attitude towards people, will girls like him? The answer is a resounding NO. And here is my reasoning; this guy will not change his attitude and he may treat his woman in the same manner. So, try changing your habit and embrace gentleness as a virtue. You will be one step towards winning the heart of some of the amazing ladies. Imagine four to five ladies fighting for you......won't you feel great?

Believe it or not, this is one of those areas that really influence how women perceive you. No woman will want to associate herself to a man who cannot even provide the simplest necessity. And I know most men understand this because most of you have ever been asked this question, "What do you do for a living?" whereas this can sound materialistic but get it down into your head that women love great things and great things can only be provided by men with stable background. Let truth be told.

I neither will nor love to hear through a forum or newspaper that some men are seeking help because they have been left by their women who claim they can't even feed them. So if you don't want this embarrassment of another man taking away your woman, then first secure your stability. This is your secret weapon; money is almost everything. In addition, be a responsible guy and accomplish all you have planned to do and see if no woman will come knocking your door.

What about the idea of being her knight in shining armor? Men, here is one more free weapon you need if you want them flock your way - be near to her during needy times. And don't get me wrong, it doesn't mean that when you are her knight in the armor that she can't do things by herself. The point here is that by doing this, it is like giving her tools that will help rescue herself from hard situations. Think of being emotionally supportive during her bad times such as after a hard day.

And if you never knew that men are gifted in finding solution, I guess you must be living in another planet. Offer emotional support and she will speak out her problems. Help her find solutions and this is the power of a man. You can still go ahead into helping her achieve what she want and be sure to reap great. So do you still want to be the lone, frustrated and groom man? I guess no. Then be this man, be supportive.

Being a jerk is not the way for you. I understand that you may be that guy women will not want to date; it may be due to your complexities, looks or anything beyond your control. Don't worry. Just be patient and keep trying. Just understand that sometimes people don't connect. You are destined for somebody. Keep searching for her. She is around the corner .Never say never until it's over. Get that into your mind and keep walking like John Walker!

Be yourself; do your own things. If you prefer staying indoors to going out to hang out with friends, be sure to be doing something constructive. Avoid hanging out waiting for them or even sending flowers now and then. You know best what you can do during this time. You can hang out with friends, hang out alone, or do things you enjoy most. This will present a good opportunity for you to develop the skills that women find attractive. What are you waiting for, this is the time for you man.

Women love freedom, don't be too into them. If you never knew that women don't love the clinging and controlling men, you have been living in the dark, and you must be pitied. Butit's not too late. You can still change if you want tremendous progress as far as attracting women is concerned.

So if you have a certain girl in mind that you are trying to fish, then show her that you can do your own things without them .Don't try to manipulate them into accompanying you top a place or constantly asking for a bout with them. Don't try to guilt them, in fact you will be annoying them by constantly asking them to hang out with you. Give them the freedom they need. Remember that they too have friends. They also hate or despise followers. Research has shown that men who imitate or try following other people don't impact on women. So if you have been a follower, stop. Instead start trends by yourself. Women love cool men with great personality. So try to act independently and show your personality. Don't just copy what other guys are doing.

Being creepy is like taking poison that will kill you. This is one of the most fundamental aspects as far as dating and getting women to follow you is concerned. Desist from making awkward statements, comments and jokes. They will greatly judge you based on your comments. Just act the cool man. Keep your eyes on her face and please don't stalk them. And if one or two girls notice that you are a creeper, chances is that all other potential girls will be warned against dating you. Don't you think this is doom? Follow this rule: don't say to a girl what you won't say to your mom. Period.

Stay independent but don't stay too independent. Don't let girls have this perception that you are too independent and you probably don't need them. God created you for them, so you need to date. Just appreciate them and one day that dream girl will be your host. In addition, you can occasionally flick or better still find ways of letting them know that you truly appreciate them and you are interested.

Just as you will not blush when this guy (or girl) comes to you in the supermarket, do the same to this gorgeous lady (or man). Don't blush. Treat her the same way as your friend and she will come for more. In other words, do not have any dating interest with anybody. I know it is hard as it sounds but that is the point. Hold that feeling back till you actually run into each other; the feelings should be mutual.

All the above tips are my idea but getting a woman interested in you is an individual initiative. Nothing will come without effort and change. You have the chance and the next time we meet you will be asking me tips on how to get rid of these women who don't want to keep their eyes off you.

8 A WORD OF WARNING

"It is possible that longing for something is better than actually having it. I've heard it said that satisfaction is the death of desire."

This book should in no way shape any future decisions you choose to make surrounding your health or happiness. If you choose to follow in the path of Mr Moody, you will almost certainly die. Hank Moody is a fictional character. You are not. The disclaimer at the beginning of the book will hopefully cover my ass for any eventuality that may result in your death, but if it doesn't, let it be known that this wasn't the way it was meant to be. I love my readers, and the last thing I want is to hear that you've killed yourself. If this does occur, please rest in peace, and assured that I'll have a drink for you on the understanding that you should have one waiting for me at the pearly gates. I expect however, we'll both be going to hell.

Living a fast life is one of the riskiest things that one can do. A person living a fast life can die at any time because he/she is always exposed to death possibilities. The modern lives that many people are living without understanding it properly has led to the increased number of people living life in the fast lane. For instance, many people are exposed to drugs, alcohol, sexual activities, robbery, etc. at a very early age. This means that these young people grow in environments that teach them how to live fast lives.

On the contrary, there are many people who think that living a fast life is exciting. This is normally portrayed in movies where main actors and actresses are seen living fast lives and be able to get nearly anything they need. But at the end of it all, it is normally said that live fast life and die faster. This is what has to be understood by those people who admire actors, actresses and artists who seem to be living in the fast lane. Most people do in the process of 'acting' and they live a completely different life in their real lives. Therefore, living life in the fast lane may appear to be attractive and exciting from the outside but in the real sense it is a life than no one can ever admire because its vulnerabilities are more than benefits, if any. What appears to be attractive in living in the fast lane is never attractive once you get there.

Starting to live fast is very easy and you may find yourself living fast without knowing. For example, when you are being raised in an environment where all your friends are doing drugs and alcohol abuse, there are higher chances of finding yourself in the same line. This is commonly referred to as peer pressure where you are influenced by your friends to start abusing drugs and alcohol. Majority of the young people normally admire the kind of fast lives that some people live without getting the real picture of what such people go through. Several studies have been conducted and many of the people living fast lives have admitted that they are never happy with the kind of lives they live. Such people confess that if only they could reverse their lives, they would do everything possible to avoid fast life.

People who are addicted to excessive alcohol consumption and drug abuse are among the most affected. These people live dangerous lives not only to themselves but also to those around them. Their health is greatly affected and there is not proper coordination of body functioning. Such people are exposed to diseases they can do anything, including having unprotected sex, once they are under influence of the substances. On the other hand, such people cannot live without the drugs and alcohol. What this means is that they can engage in robbery with violence just to get money to buy the drugs or alcohol. One of the major affect groups from drug addicts and heavy drinkers is their families. Once this group start living fast life, they abandon their families and even start selling home properties just to have money for drinking or buying drugs. Therefore, alcoholics and drug abusers are exposed to numerous diseases (such as cancer, brain damage, liver disease, heart attacks, STIs, endless hangovers, etc.) and even death. This is even worse especially for women.

People living life in the fast lane normally lack good morals and they end up engaging in risky behaviors of irresponsible sexual acts. These people live reckless lives and engage themselves in activities that put their health at risk in very easy ways. Such people can sleep with anybody regardless of their status. This is mainly because they think that living life in the fast lane is glamorous and that when they sleep with multiple partners then they become conquerors. What they do not understand that such behaviors only expose their health to risk and that they can contract disease anyhow. Many have contracted AIDs through such irresponsible sexual acts and they have ended up dying in the name of living life in the fast lane.

It is also common for people living life in the fast lane to end up in prison due to their illegal activities. Definitely you should expect people selling drugs, abusing the drugs or consuming excess alcohol to be doing so against the law. Most of the countries prohibit sale and use of certain drugs such as heroin, cocaine, bhang, etc. Nevertheless, most of those living fast lives use such drugs which are illegal. This means that this group is always hiding from the authorities because they know that they are engaging in illegal businesses and deals. But at the end of it, majority of them get arrested and put behind bars for the rest of their lives. Unfortunately, some end up being shot while on the chase by the police. This implies that such people will always live in fear of being arrested and that they will never have a peace of mind throughout their lives since they also understand that the authorities are ever after them.

It is also very common to find different groups of

people living fast lives fighting each other. In most cases, it may be due to disagreement on deals or fight for customers to purchase their illegal drugs. As a result of this, they end up creating hatred amongst themselves. After sometime, they will start opposing each other leading to fights and lastly killings. That is why you hear of illegal groups opening fire at each other in certain places of the world. This means that these people are enemies of each other and they can turn against each other at any time; which is very dangerous.

People living lives in the fast lane are always after becoming rich and famous. As a result of this, they can do anything to get what they want in life. In fact majority of them engage in illegal activities even if it means satanic activities or criminal acts. In most cases, they become criminals, rapists, devil worshippers, fraudsters, etc. just to get more money and fame. Unfortunately, they use the money and fame they get wrongly. For example, males will use the money to attract females and engage in multiple unprotected sexual activities hence putting their lives at risk. Therefore in general, this group of people is dangerous even to the society as a whole because it is the society that they rob and kill.

The group of people living life in the fast lane is dangerous to the society as a whole. This calls for everyone's participation if this has to be changed. The first thing to be done is to mobilize these groups and inform them about the reality of life. It is strange to find that most of them admire and copy the living in the fast lane lifestyles from movies they watch and artists they come across. They do not understand that such movie stars do so while acting only and it is not their real life. It is very unfortunate for those who imitate what they see in movies and practice them in their real lives.

Establishment of rehabilitation centers can be one of the most reliable ways to help people living in the fast lane. Some find themselves in such scenarios as a result of peer influence and the environments where they live. But when they realize what they want to achieve in life, they are always willing to change their lifestyles and live in reality. Therefore such groups can be assisted by being taken to rehabilitation centers and slowly helped to get out of the fast lane lives. It is wrong to see those living fast lives as people who cannot change and who should be completely eliminated from the society. This can only worsen the situation and the appropriate action is to develop positive attitude towards them and try to impact their lives positively.

Another reason as to why people find themselves living in the fast lane is idleness. It is said that 'an idle mind is a devils workshop' and this is what normally leads to some people to start thinking of living fast. When such people find themselves doing nothing at all at all times, they can easily be brainwashed into bad behavior such as excessive consumption of alcohol, crimes and robbery, irresponsible sexual activities, drug abuse, etc. One of the major contributions is unemployment. This is a global challenge because there are high unemployment rates in nearly all parts of the world. The efforts of the unemployed persons can be easily directed to living in the fast lane because such groups get attracted with the so called exciting lives that are exhibited by those believed to be living in the fast lane.

Therefore governments should also come up with strategies that will create employment opportunities to as many people as possible so that the number of idlers can be reduced across the world. In fact such idleness is what makes it easier to convince youths to join terrorist groups and become dangerous to the world.

Parents, counselors, religious leaders, non-governmental organizations, etc. should also join hands in instilling good morals to young people. Research has shown that children who receive good parenting are less likely to be easily convinced by their peers to engage in risky behaviors. By encouraging parents to use the right methods and channels to teach their children about good morals, cases of living in the fast lane can be greatly reduced.

The truth of the matter is that people who live in the fast lane lack good morals and they always live in risky environments. They never appreciate the aspect of responsible behaviors but one thing about them is that they do not understand themselves completely. Majority of them live the kind of lives they live as a result of peer influence, poor parental care, greed for quick money, etc. Something that should be understood is that people living in the fast lane not only risky they lives but also the lives of those around them. Therefore when we look at it in a wider perspective, everybody can be affected by the kind of lives these people are living. For example, when such people plan to steal it is very rare for them to steal from their colleagues but they will plan to rob the society as a whole. Thus everybody's life is put at risk, in one way or another, as a result of people living life in the fast lane. This is a dangerous group of people to everybody.

It is also very easy to become addicted in living in the fast lane. The ease of addiction is normally high in youths and women. It is for this reason that makes it very challenging to get such people out of their fast lane lives. Thus when attempting to help such people get out of their fast lane lives, proper measures have to be put in place because it is always a difficult task.

A change cannot be made unless an action plan is made and action taken. Living in the fast lane only reduces your days of living because you will never be in a safe environment. As a matter of fact, all that you will be surrounded with are diseases, risky behaviors, and chances of dying. By living in the fast lane, it only means that death can get you anytime anywhere. Therefore it is important to develop good morals and accept the reality of life which is to live a positive life. In most cases, good things that come very quickly and through illegal means never last and they only endanger your life. Don't be a dick.

Californication returns in 2014 for a seventh season.

ABOUT THE AUTHOR

L. A. Moore lives in the UK and drives a Porsche 911.

83712249R00053

Made in the USA
Lexington, KY
14 March 2018